Franz Joseph Haydn

Missa in Tempore Belli

Mass in Time of War/ 'Paukenmesse'

VOCAL SCORE

Edited by

DAVID RUSSELL HULME

MUSIC DEPARTMENT

OXFORD

UNIVERSITY PRESS

OXFORD
UNIVERSITY PRESS

Great Clarendon Street, Oxford OX2 6DP, England
198 Madison Avenue, New York, NY10016, USA

Oxford University Press is a department of the University of Oxford.
It furthers the University's aim of excellence in research, scholarship,
and education by publishing worldwide

Oxford is a registered trade mark of Oxford University Press
in the UK and in certain other countries

© Oxford University Press 2002

The moral rights of the author have been asserted
Database right Oxford University Press (maker)

First published 2002

5 7 9 10 8 6

ISBN 0-19-336792-0

Music origination by Woodrow,
Printed in Great Britain on acid-free paper by
Caligraving Ltd., Thetford, Norfolk.

The full score (with critical commentary) and orchestral material are available for hire from the publisher's hire library.

Scoring:
original (Eisenstadt) version—SATB (soli and tutti); 2 oboes, 2 clarinets, 2 bassoons, 2 horns, 2 trumpets,
timpani, strings, and organ continuo.

expanded (Vienna) version—as above with the addition of flute and expanded parts for clarinets and horns (see Preface).

Duration: *c*.40 mins

CONTENTS

PREFACE

Following a brilliantly successful second visit to London, Haydn returned to Vienna in the autumn of 1795 to resume his duties as Kappellmeister to the Esterhàzy family. The court orchestra, disbanded by Prince Anton, had been re-established by the new prince, Nicolaus II, but the demands on Haydn were to be relatively limited. Thus he was able to settle permanently in the city and concentrate his court attendance into a few summer and autumn months at Eisenstadt, where the court was then based.

Prince Nicolaus II had a particular enthusiasm for church music, and the most important requirement of his Kappellmeister was the composition each year of a new mass for the name day of his wife, Princess Josepha Maria. The *Missa in Tempore Belli* was almost certainly the first in the magnificent series of six masses—collectively known as the *Hermenegild* masses—which Haydn composed for this purpose between 1796 and 1802. In the years following his return to Vienna until his death in 1809, choral music came to dominate the composer's output and, together with *The Creation* (1798) and *The Seasons* (1801), these late masses represent the crowning glory of Haydn's final creative period.

Title and first performance
By the time Haydn arrived back in Vienna in 1795, the Austro-Hungarian empire was at war with France and suffering heavy defeats from the advancing troops under the leadership of the brilliant young General Bonaparte. It was during these dark days that the composer began work on a new mass. He dated the manuscript 1796 and headed it with the title *Missa in Tempore Belli*—'Mass in Time of War'. Thoughts of battle must have undoubtedly been in his mind as he wrote the 'Agnus Dei', with its martial trumpets and drums, and ominous, quiet timpani patterns which eventually gave rise to the mass's popular German title *Paukenmesse*— 'Kettledrum Mass'. Both this mass and the *Missa St Bernardi* were begun in 1796, but there is some uncertainty over which was first performed that year and which the next. A new Haydn mass was certainly heard in the Piaristenkirche in Vienna on St Stephen's Day (26 December) 1796; Robbins Landon's discovery of contemporary parts of the *Missa in Tempore Belli* in the church archives strongly suggests that this was the work performed on that day and unveiled at Eisenstadt the previous September.

Scoring
Haydn's autograph, now in the Esterhàzy Archive, Budapest, contains parts for soprano, alto, tenor, and bass voices (solo and chorus), 2 oboes, 2 clarinets, 2 bassoons, 2 horns, 2 trumpets (*clarini*), 2 timpani, violin I, violin II, viola, cello, double bass, and organ continuo. The clarinets only appear in the 'Credo', and the horns only in the 'Et incarnatus' section of the 'Credo'. There are some indications in the manuscript for flute in the 'Qui tollis' but these are not in Haydn's hand. Fortunately, the orchestral material survives from the first Eisenstadt performance—having spent many years up a chimney, where it was hidden from Russian troops who invaded the castle in 1945—and confirms that a flute was not included on that occasion. However, a part for flute, and expanded contributions from the clarinets and horns, appear in the authoritative parts (which carry Haydn's holograph corrections) preserved in the archive of the Hofmusik-Kapelle in Vienna. Clearly, Haydn decided to augment the scoring when the mass was performed in Vienna, and in all probability he did so for the very first performance at the Piaristenkirche.

The additional parts for horns simply duplicate those for trumpets throughout (but, being in C *basso*, sound an octave lower). The flute, too, primarily doubles; in this case, the solo cello line for part of the 'Qui tollis'. The clarinet parts are certainly the most significant of the additions, containing independent strands at a number of telling moments (e.g. 'Gloria', bars 8–12, and 'Sanctus', bars 28–30).

Early and modern editions
The first published edition of the mass was issued *circa* 1803 by Breitkopf and Härtel of Leipzig. Although produced with Haydn's permission, it is not consistently reliable and contains numerous corruptions and questionable articulation instructions. The full score follows the Vienna instrumentation insofar as it includes flute in the 'Qui tollis' and has horns doubling trumpets throughout, but it omits the additional parts for clarinets. This edition

defined the standard performing text for over one hundred and fifty years, and was the basis for the orchestral parts issued by Novello of London and the same publisher's vocal score of *circa* 1878 that is still in use today.

Robbins Landon's *urtext* for the Joseph Haydn-Institut, Cologne, complete edition, appeared in 1958. (*Joseph Haydn-Werke*, Reihe XXIII, Band 2: *Messen Nr 5–8* Munich–Duisburg, 1958). Derived from the composer's autograph and other authoritative early sources and edited with unerring integrity, it was a revelation. However, the supplementary parts for clarinets and horns were authenticated too late to be incorporated into the full score, although a flute does appear in the 'Qui tollis'. The miniature score of the same edition issued by Bärenreiter in 1961 was able to include the clarinet parts in an appendix. These figure in the piano reduction printed in the 1962 Bärenreiter vocal score, which was published to complement the collected edition.

The present edition

This is the first critical edition prepared from Haydn's autograph manuscript to fully integrate the expanded Viennese scoring. The full score and orchestral parts present the material in a way that indicates clearly what was included in the original working and what was added later. The piano reduction in the vocal score identifies material present only in the Viennese version and prints it in cue-sized notation. Thus, performers may choose either the original Eisenstadt scoring or the later and fuller Viennese alternative. Both are equally authoritative and effective.

Haydn's intentions regarding articulation, dynamics, and other performance instructions are neither completely, nor clearly and consistently, notated in his autograph manuscript. The present edition has drawn judicious analogies to produce a text that is both musically consistent and practical. Such editorial intervention is identified in the full score and/or the associated critical commentary but is not differentiated in the vocal score or the orchestral parts. The editor has refrained from incorporating stylistic suggestions without specific textual justification, except for the few vocal slurs that appear as broken slurs in the vocal score. The rationale behind these suggestions lies in Haydn's use of slurs to indicate articulation in his vocal lines and, in particular, the common appearance of slurs in moving parts that set a single syllable simultaneously with its

appearance against a single note in one or more other voices. Examples are found in the 'Gloria', bars 94 and 98, and the 'Credo', bars 79 and 81, and the practice is particularly common between a dominant and its approach chord at cadences such as we find in the 'Gloria', bars 219 and 268. These editorial suggestions have been made with due consideration to the musical context and effect and performers should feel free to adopt or reject them—or add others following like principles. (Broken slurs appear in instrumental parts and vocal score where they have been included by analogy with broken slurs in the voice parts.) It was common practice for Haydn and many composers of the eighteenth and nineteenth centuries to omit vocal dynamics for solo sections. None are found in the manuscript of the *Missa in Tempore Belli* and none have been added in this edition.

The piano reduction, newly prepared for this vocal score, aims to present a reasonably full representation of the instrumental textures whilst remaining comfortably practical for the keyboard player. All ornaments and grace notes have been tacitly slurred into principal notes in all the performing material. Similarly, where Haydn's manuscript does not slur trills into the note(s) following, slurs have been tacitly added to achieve this. Appoggiaturas generally appear in the manuscript as quaver grace notes irrespective of their intended length. They have been realized in both the vocal score and orchestral parts but are differentiated by the use of cue-sized noteheads. The editor has adopted the readings given in the Breitkopf and Härtel full score, published less than ten years after the mass was composed, accepting them as reliable indications of contemporary performance practice. As in several other of his mass settings, Haydn omits part of the full liturgical text within the 'Credo' and 'Et resurrexit' sections. Punctuation, capitalization, and syllabic division of the Latin text follow modern practice.

David Russell Hulme
Aberystwyth 2002

Missa in Tempore Belli

Mass in Time of War / 'Paukenmesse'

Kyrie

Edited by
David Russell Hulme

JOSEPH HAYDN (1732–1809)
Hob. XXII. 9

Allegro moderato

SOPRANO SOLO

* For significance of small noteheads see Preface.

(Stand →)

6

SOPRANO SOLO

Ky - ri - e____ e - lei - son, e - lei - son,

12

Gloria

S. Do - mi - ne Fi - li u - ni - ge - ni - te Je - su

A. Do - mi - ne Fi - li u - ni - ge - ni - te Je - su

T. Do - mi - ne Fi - li u - ni - ge - ni - te

B. Do - mi - ne Fi - li u - ni - ge - ni - te

Chri - ste, Je - su Chri - ste.

Chri - ste, Je - su Chri - ste.

Je - su, Je - su Chri - ste.

Je - su, Je - su Chri - ste.

* Haydn's autograph full score gives both
notes, but indicates no preference.

†

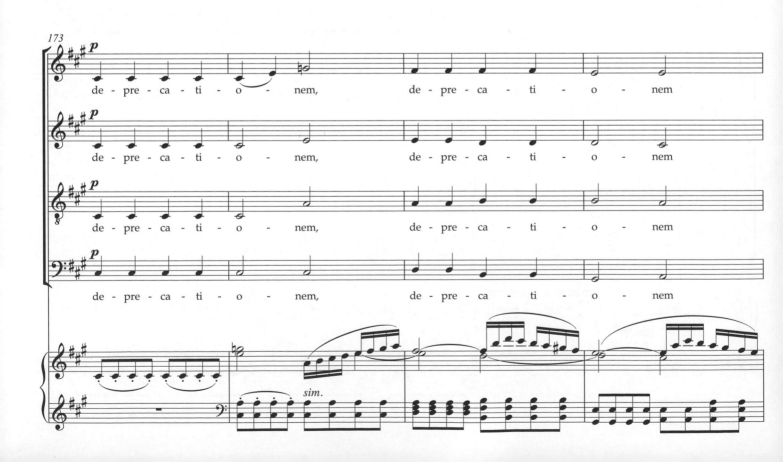

Credo

34

se - det ad dex - te - ram Pa - - - tris.

se - det ad dex - te - ram Pa - - - tris.

se - det ad dex - te - ram Pa - - - tris.

se - det ad dex - te - ram Pa - - - tris.

Et i - te - rum ven - tu - rus est cum glo - ri - a

Et i - te - rum ven - tu - rus est cum glo - ri - a

Et i - te - rum ven - tu - rus est cum glo - ri - a

Et i - te - rum ven - tu - rus est cum glo - ri - a

42

44

52

Sanctus

Do - mi - nus De - us Sa - ba - oth,   Do - mi - nus De - us Sa - - - - - ba-

Do - mi - nus De - us Sa - ba - oth,   Do - mi - nus De - us Sa - - - - - ba-

Do - mi - nus De - us Sa - ba - oth,   Do - mi - nus De - us Sa - - - - - ba-

Do - mi - nus De - us Sa - ba - oth,   Do - mi - nus De - us Sa - - - - - ba-

-oth.   Ple - ni sunt cae - li et ter - - ra,

-oth.   Ple - ni sunt cae - li et ter - - ra,

-oth.   Ple - ni sunt cae - li et ter - - ra,

-oth.   Ple - ni sunt cae - li et ter - - - - - - ra,

Benedictus

Agnus Dei